EXPLORING COUNTRIES

South Africa

by Lisa Owings

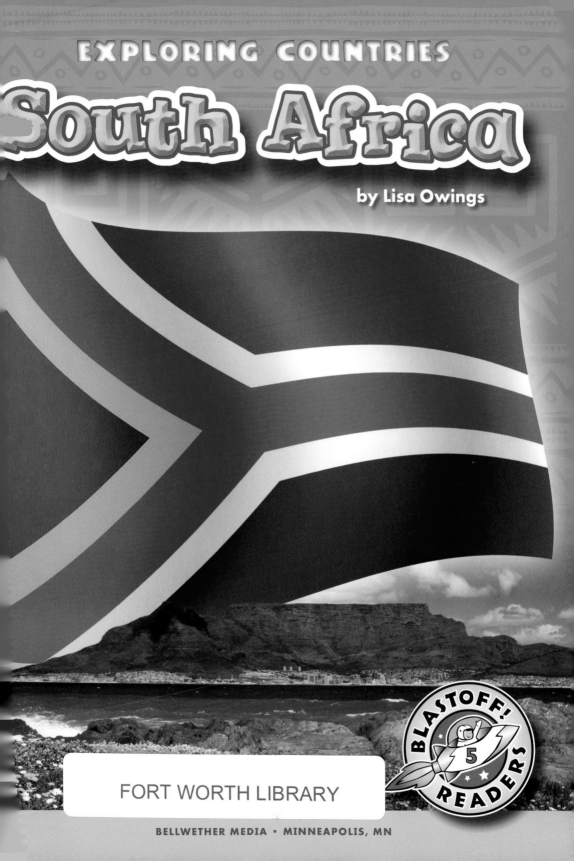

FORT WORTH LIBRARY

BELLWETHER MEDIA · MINNEAPOLIS, MN

Note to Librarians, Teachers, and Parents:

Blastoff! Readers are carefully developed by literacy experts and combine standards-based content with developmentally appropriate text.

Level 1 provides the most support through repetition of high-frequency words, light text, predictable sentence patterns, and strong visual support.

Level 2 offers early readers a bit more challenge through varied simple sentences, increased text load, and less repetition of high-frequency words.

Level 3 advances early-fluent readers toward fluency through increased text and concept load, less reliance on visuals, longer sentences, and more literary language.

Level 4 builds reading stamina by providing more text per page, increased use of punctuation, greater variation in sentence patterns, and increasingly challenging vocabulary.

Level 5 encourages children to move from "learning to read" to "reading to learn" by providing even more text, varied writing styles, and less familiar topics.

Whichever book is right for your reader, Blastoff! Readers are the perfect books to build confidence and encourage a love of reading that will last a lifetime!

This edition first published in 2012 by Bellwether Media, Inc.

No part of this publication may be reproduced in whole or in part without written permission of the publisher. For information regarding permission, write to Bellwether Media, Inc., Attention: Permissions Department, 5357 Penn Avenue South, Minneapolis, MN 55419.

Library of Congress Cataloging-in-Publication Data
Owings, Lisa.
South Africa / by Lisa Owings.
   p. cm. – (Blastoff! readers) (Exploring countries)
Includes bibliographical references and index.
Summary: "Developed by literacy experts for students in grades three through seven, this book introduces young readers to the geography and culture of South Africa"–Provided by publisher.
ISBN 978-1-60014-623-7 (hardcover : alk. paper)
 1. South Africa–Juvenile literature. I. Title.
DT1719.O95 2011
968–dc22
                    2011002227

Printed in the United States of America, North Mankato, MN.

080111   1187

Contents

Where Is South Africa?   4
The Land   6
The Cape Floral Kingdom   8
Wildlife   10
The People   12
Daily Life   14
Going to School   16
Working   18
Playing   20
Food   22
Holidays   24
The Rainbow Nation   26
Fast Facts   28
Glossary   30
To Learn More   31
Index   32

Zimbabwe

Botswana

Namibia

Pretoria ⭐

Bloemfontein ⭐

Lesotho

South Africa

Cape Town
⭐

Atlantic
Ocean

Did you know?

Prince Edward Island and Marion Island are also part of South Africa. These small islands lie about 1,200 miles (1,931 kilometers) southeast of Cape Town.

Mozambique

Swaziland

Indian
Ocean

N

W E

S

South Africa lies on the southern tip of Africa. It covers 470,693 square miles (1,219,090 square kilometers). The Atlantic Ocean meets the country's western coast. The waves of the Indian Ocean wash onto the eastern shore. South Africa shares its northern border with Namibia, Botswana, and Zimbabwe. Mozambique and Swaziland lie to the east. Lesotho is a small country within South Africa. Unlike most other countries, South Africa has three capital cities. Pretoria is the main capital. The other capitals are Cape Town and Bloemfontein.

A large **plateau** covers most of South Africa. It rises up to 8,000 feet (2,438 meters) above the surrounding land. Dry, grassy plains fill most of the plateau. Trees and bushes grow in the northeast. To the west lie sandy deserts.

A stretch of land called the Great **Escarpment** separates the plateau from the coast. The eastern part of this land is called the Drakensberg, or Dragon Mountains. The Orange River flows from these mountains. It is the longest river in South Africa. Its waters rush westward and plunge over the mighty Augrabies Falls.

Did you know?
The flat-topped mountain overlooking Cape Town is a symbol of South Africa. Its shape earned it the name Table Mountain.

Table Mountain

7

king protea

South Africa is one of the few countries that has a **floral kingdom**. The Cape Floral Kingdom lies along the Atlantic coast and has around 9,000 different kinds of plants. About 6,300 grow nowhere else in the world. Most of the plants are *fynbos*, or "fine bush," plants. *Fynbos* plants have hard, narrow leaves. The king protea, South Africa's national flower, is a *fynbos* plant.

Next to the Cape Floral Kingdom lie the deserts of Namaqualand. Millions of seeds wait beneath the sand for rain. When rain comes each spring, the desert sand becomes a carpet of colorful blooms. These flowers bring visitors from around the world to South Africa.

leopard

blue crane

black mamba

fun fact

One out of every four snakes in South Africa is poisonous. The venom of the black mamba can kill a person in less than an hour!

South Africa is home to some of the largest animals in the world. Huge elephants and rhinoceroses rumble across the plains. Lions, leopards, and wild dogs chase zebras and antelope. Giraffes use their long necks to reach the leaves of tall trees. In rivers and lakes, hippopotamuses lurk in the water.

Did you know?
Great white sharks swim and hunt off the coast of South Africa. They are one of the deadliest animals in the world!

great white shark

Smaller animals live throughout South Africa, too. Boomslangs, black mambas, and other snakes wrap themselves around tree branches. The rare riverine rabbit survives only in the country's dry, western **scrublands**. Hundreds of different birds add color to South Africa's landscape. Eagles, parrots, kingfishers, and bee-eaters fly in search of food. The blue crane is South Africa's national bird.

South Africa is a country with **diverse** peoples and languages. Over 49 million people call the country home. About 8 out of every 10 are black Africans. Some are **descendants** of the San, the first people to live in South Africa. Most are descendants of the Bantu peoples who arrived thousands of years after the San.

White South Africans have mainly Dutch or British **ancestors**. A small number of people come from India and Asia. Some South Africans also have mixed backgrounds. South Africa has 11 official languages. Zulu, Xhosa, and Afrikaans are the most widely spoken. English is used by the government and media.

Speak Zulu!

English	Zulu	How to say it
hello	sawubona	sow-BOH-nah
good-bye (leaving)	sala kahle	SAH-lah gah-they
good-bye (staying)	hamba kahle	HAM-bah gah-they
yes	yebo	YEH-boh
no	cha	tah
please	ngicela	ngee-TREH-lah
thank you	ngiyabonga	ngee-yah-BOHN-gah
friend	mngani	oom-GAH-neh

Life in South African cities is different than life in the countryside. The cities buzz with activity. Some South Africans have large houses or apartments. They use cars to get around. Many South Africans cannot afford houses or apartments. They build homes out of pieces of wood and metal. They ride small buses to get from place to place.

Most South Africans in the countryside live in small villages or on farms. Many do not have electricity or running water. People walk or bike around their villages. They can take a bus or taxi into town. Small shops, outdoor markets, and street stands sell goods to villagers and travelers.

Where People Live in South Africa

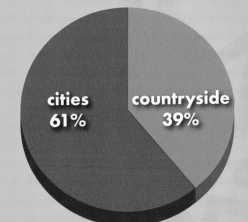

cities 61%

countryside 39%

Did you know?

Many South Africans in the countryside still live like their ancestors did. They have homes made of mud and reeds, and some still wear traditional clothing.

Children in South Africa begin school at age 7. They are required to attend through ninth grade. Students take classes in math, science, social studies, art, and physical education. Around half of all South African students stay in school through grade twelve. In grades ten through twelve, they continue to study math and science. They also study business and other subjects to help them prepare for careers. Those who graduate must pass an exam if they want to attend one of South Africa's many colleges and universities. Students who do not pass can still attend a **vocational school**.

Did you know?

Each school teaches classes in the language of the region. It is important for South Africans to learn more than one language. Students begin to learn English and other languages as early as first grade.

fun fact

Many South Africans make and sell artwork. Some skilled artists create beautiful works of art out of scrap metal or plastic shopping bags.

South Africans work many different jobs. Most people in cities have **service jobs**. They work in schools, banks, offices, shops, and restaurants. Hotel workers serve a growing number of **tourists**. Factory workers make food products, metals, **textiles**, and chemicals. These products are shipped around the world.

Miners and farmers work in the countryside. Miners bring up gold and diamonds from deep in the earth. They also dig up coal and iron ore. Farmers grow grains, sugarcane, fruits, and vegetables. Cows, sheep, pigs, and chickens are also raised throughout the country.

Where People Work in South Africa

manufacturing
23%

services 72%

farming
5%

Did you know?

In 2010, South Africa hosted the World Cup. It was the first time this soccer tournament had been held in Africa.

South Africans enjoy a wide variety of activities. Soccer is the most popular sport in the country. Rugby, cricket, and track-and-field are other favorite sports. South Africans also enjoy exploring the outdoors. People can hike trails, climb mountains, and spot wildlife in the country's national parks. Swimmers and fishermen can often be found off the coast.

South Africans also love music and dance. Different age groups enjoy different styles of music. Older South Africans enjoy traditional African music and dancing. Hip hop has become popular with young people. Teenagers go with friends to concerts and dance parties.

Did you know?

South Africans often enjoy a traditional outdoor barbeque called a braai.

braai

South Africans enjoy a wide variety of foods. Corn is used in many traditional African dishes. Cornmeal **porridge** called *mealie pap* is common. For a dish called *umngqusho*, dried corn is pounded and mixed with beans, butter, onions, potatoes, chilies, and lemon. Corn on the cob is roasted and sold as a snack.

Dutch and British dishes in South Africa usually feature meat with potatoes or rice. Sausages called *boerewors* and dried strips of meat called *biltong* are favorites. The country is also famous for a sweet dessert called *melktert*. It is a pastry with a filling made from milk, flour, sugar, and eggs.

melktert

boerewors

Freedom Day

Many national holidays celebrate events in
South Africa's history. April 27 is Freedom Day.
On this day in 1994, South Africans voted in the first
election of their new **democracy**. Thousands gather
in Pretoria to enjoy music, dancing, and speeches.
On September 24, people celebrate Heritage
Day. This honors the diversity of South Africa.

Most South Africans celebrate Christmas and New Year's. For Christmas, families have a *braai* and exchange gifts. People often celebrate New Year's with picnics and trips to the beach. The next day, many South Africans dress in costumes and dance in the streets.

fun fact

The Cape Town International Kite Festival is the largest kite festival in Africa. It draws around 25,000 people every year and features beautiful kites from around the world.

New Year's

South Africans are proud of their diversity. They call their country the Rainbow Nation. Before 1994, however, South Africans lived under a system called **apartheid**. Non-white South Africans had to live, work, and go to school in areas separate from white South Africans. After many years, laws were passed to end apartheid. Today, every South African has to be treated with **equality**.

Nelson Mandela

F.W. de Klerk

In 1993, Nelson Mandela and F.W. de Klerk won the Nobel Peace Prize for their work to end apartheid. Mandela became president of South Africa in 1994. Since then, the country has continued to grow as a democracy. Its people are learning to live together in peace. They are teaching the world that what we have in common is more important than what we do not.

South Africa's Flag

A sideways "Y" sits in the center of South Africa's flag. The arms of the "Y" hold a black triangle outlined in yellow. The rest of the "Y" is outlined in white and separates a red stripe on top from a blue stripe on the bottom. The colors of the flag stand for the peoples of South Africa. The design of the flag represents all South Africans coming together in peace. This flag was adopted in 1994 as a symbol of the new democracy.

Official Name: Republic of South Africa

Area: 470,693 square miles
(1,219,090 square kilometers);
South Africa is the 25th largest
country in the world.

Capital Cities:	Pretoria, Bloemfontein, Cape Town
Important Cities:	Johannesburg, Durban, Port Elizabeth
Population:	49,004,031 (July 2011)
Official Languages:	Zulu, Xhosa, Afrikaans, Sepedi, English, Setswana, Sesotho, Xitsonga, Ndebele, Tshivenda, Swati
National Holiday:	Freedom Day (April 27)
Religions:	Christian (79.7%), None (15.1%) Other (5.2%)
Major Industries:	farming, fishing, manufacturing, mining, services
Natural Resources:	gold, diamonds, coal, iron ore, platinum, copper, salt, natural gas
Manufactured Products:	metals, machinery, clothing, chemicals, fertilizers, food products
Farm Products:	corn, wheat, vegetables, fruits, sugarcane, wool, dairy products, beef, poultry
Unit of Money:	rand; the rand is divided into 100 cents.

Glossary

ancestors—relatives who lived long ago

apartheid—a system of racial separation that once existed in South Africa; non-whites were separated from whites and treated differently based on their race; apartheid ended in 1994.

democracy—a form of government in which people choose their leaders

descendants—people related to a person or group of people who lived long ago

diverse—varied; South Africans come from diverse backgrounds.

equality—sameness

escarpment—a long cliff or steep slope formed by erosion; the Great Escarpment was formed by rivers in South Africa's coastal plains.

floral kingdom—one of six areas of the world recognized for unique plant life; the Cape Floral Kingdom in South Africa is the smallest and richest floral kingdom in the world.

plateau—an area of flat, raised land

porridge—a food made by boiling grains in milk or water

scrublands—areas of land that are densely covered with small bushes and trees

service jobs—jobs that perform tasks for people or businesses

textiles—fabrics or clothes that have been woven or knitted

tourists—people who are visiting a country

vocational school—a school that trains students to do specific jobs

To Learn More

AT THE LIBRARY

Blauer, Ettagale, and Jason Lauré. *South Africa.* New York, N.Y.: Children's Press, 2006.

Mace, Virginia. *South Africa.* Washington, D.C.: National Geographic, 2008.

Van Wyk, Chris. *Nelson Mandela: Long Walk to Freedom.* New York, N.Y.: Macmillan, 2009.

ON THE WEB

Learning more about South Africa is as easy as 1, 2, 3.

1. Go to www.factsurfer.com.

2. Enter "South Africa" into the search box.

3. Click the "Surf" button and you will see a list of related Web sites.

With factsurfer.com, finding more information is just a click away.

Index

activities, 20, 21

apartheid, 26, 27

Bloemfontein, 4, 5

Cape Floral Kingdom, 8-9

Cape Town, 4, 5, 7, 25

capitals (see Bloemfontein,
    Cape Town, and Pretoria)

daily life, 14-15

de Klerk, F.W., 27

Drakensberg, 7

education, 16-17

food, 22-23

Freedom Day, 24

Great Escarpment, 7

Heritage Day, 24

holidays, 24-25

housing, 14, 15

landscape, 6-9

languages, 13, 17

location, 4-5

Mandela, Nelson, 27

Namaqualand, 9

Orange River, 7

peoples, 12-13

Pretoria, 4, 5, 24

San, 12

sports, 20

Table Mountain, 7

transportation, 14, 15

wildlife, 10-11

working, 18-19

The images in this book are reproduced through the courtesy of: Juan Martinez, front cover, pp. 6, 7, 8-9, 20; Maisei Raman, front cover (flag), p. 28; Maggie Rosier, pp. 4-5; Roder de la Harpe / Photolibrary, p. 8 (small); Michael Wick, p. 10 (top); Neil Bradfield, p. 10 (middle); Lynn M. Stone / Minden Pictures, p. 10 (bottom); Klein – Hubert / Kimballstock, pp. 10-11; Oliver Gerhard / Age Fotostock, p. 12; Stefan Espenhahn / Photolibrary, p. 14; Luke Schmidt, p. 15; Feije Riemersma / Alamy, pp. 16-17; Sylvain Grandadam / Age Fotostock, p. 18; Franz Marc Frei / Glow Images, p. 19 (left); Jim West / Alamy, p. 19 (right); Gerald Hoberman / Photolibrary, pp. 21, 22; Elzbieta Sekowska, p. 23 (left); Monkey Business Images, p. 23 (right); Adil Bradlow / AP Images, p. 24; Eric Nathan / Getty Images, p. 25; Schalk Van Zuydam / AP Images, p. 25 (small); Peter Beavis / Getty Images, pp. 26-27; Gerard Julien / Getty Images, p. 27 (small); Jonathan Noden-Wilkinson, p. 29 (bill); Kevin Fourie, p. 29 (coin).